MW01278035

COLOPHON

Set in Van Dijck, a version designed by
Jan van Krimpen (1935) of the Dutch typecutter
Cristoffel Van Dijck (1601-69). Van Dijck was a
great craftsmen of the 17th century and later
influence on William Caslon. Van Krimpen based
his roman on a specimen which was used for
a 1671 edition of Ovid printed in Amsterdam.
The italic comes from a 1660 specimen and is perhaps
more historically accurate to the Baroque style.

Titling is National Old Style
by F.W.G.

•

Book design by J. Bryan

Born in New York in 1928, Gene Frumkin is a professor emeritus of English at University of New Mexico, where he served from 1966-1994. He lived in the Bronx where his first poem was a spontaneous couplet in Yiddish at age four. When he was ten, his family moved to Los Angeles. He received his B.A. in English from the University of California at Los Angeles in 1950. After graduation, he started writing poetry. In 1966 he began a teaching career at the University of New Mexico in Albuquerque. Primarily a poet, he has also written and published fiction, reviews, and criticism. His work in poetry has been influenced at various times by his first mentor, Thomas McGrath, and later by Black Mountain, surrealism, language writing, although he claims no particular affiliation (as schools of writing) with any of these. His books include *The Old Man Who Swam Away and Left Only His Wet Feet*; *Comma in the Ear*; *Falling into Meditation*; *Saturn Is Mostly Weather: Selected & Uncollected Poems*; *Doestoevsky and Other Nature Poems*; *A Sweetness in the Air*; *Clouds and Red Earth*.

Note RE my 4-year-old oral spontaneous poem on seeing an unclothed mannikin in a store window while riding in my Uncle Joe's car during a heavy snowfall in NYC:

> Es schnait und es draight
> Und a Nacketer mann shteit
>
> It's snowing and blowing
> and a naked man is standing

Freud by Other Means

Freud by Other Means

Gene Frumkin

LA ALAMEDA PRESS   ALBUQUERQUE

To the L)edge Poets, who have been very helpful in getting
these poems to the publishing stage: Mary Rising Higgins,
David M. Johnson, Kathleen Linnell, Jeanne Shannon,
Maryhelen Snyder, Phyllis Hoge Thompson, John Tritica
and to Todd Moore, with whom I was having one of our
Monday morning breakfasts when the Freud idea
popped out of my pancakes.

Thanks to *The Best American Poetry 2002*; *Facture*; *Hambone*;
Harwood Review; *Instress Press*; *Soho*; and *Sulfur*
for publishing some of these poems prior to this publication.

Cover painting:
"The Family" — Lydia Samuels Frumkin (1938-1981)
oil on masonite

Endpiece photograph:
Greek Archaic statuette from Asia Minor (530-510 B.C.)
Barbier-Mueller Museum, Geneva, Switzerland

ISBN: 1-888809-32-9

Library of Congress #: 2002011917

La Alameda Press
9636 Guadalupe Trail NW
Albuquerque, New Mexico 87114

Contents

. . . death instincts are by their nature mute and . . .
the clamor of life proceeds for the most part from Eros.

SIGMUND FREUD
The Ego and the Id

The Life of Eternity

Most of eternity hides
in the past, sullen as black
                    ink.
          A molecule of it
       is history. The doctor
allowed himself to drift backward
as if there he could find
                 a peach
       older than Greek mythology,
            but keeping fresh
the juice of what we have always
              dreamt.

          Even in his wildest patients
he has never seen the timeless.
As he aged, the doctor visualized
     civilization as a place
        of vindictive loss.
           Creation is modest and
                vain.
Psychoanalysis, over a hundred
              years old,
          is young
        as any June butterfly.
   In the scheme of eternity
everyone will die. To keep the mind
       in its gray box, almost safe,
              almost mad,
      is a minor occupation
among the gathering stars.

As a medical man, he knew how
the eyes of humankind blink on
                and off
        as if they too
traveled great distances
around a particular god.
        Somewhere else on another
                planet,
        oxygen, if any, might have
dissipated, and people
are not human, might not breathe,
                their sky solid
        as a cinder block,
they, evanescent as smoke.

Civilization, the doctor thought,
        is only what we think it is,
                the mind
        a bowl of cherries
        practical as a roller coaster.
History is more famous
than the future, having lived longer
        in crystal and blood.

A beetle climbs the wall of
                its home.
                unhurried.
        a form of bric-a-brac,
        too lazy to care.
        Ego is our cooked goose,
the doctor explained in his writings,
his vision of dispute and discontent.

How much eternity
remains to us who imagine it
as a holy distance,
a forever of incompleteness?
Enough for God's lifetime
Enough.

Escalator

The escalator
is a dangerous enemy
who could trip you
one step at a time.
This is how the mind works,
synthesizing dream with substance.
Or as Jung
alternates
with Freud.
The substitution
of ground for holiness
claims voice as a reason
for old tribes locating
the sun
as figures
in the act, at the window.

The future derives
from sleep, evolves into gods
and animals.
This is a process
that F. chilled into
vintage prose.
Jung warmed
to the blooded world,
not alone. The human collective
describes the enormity
of a single voice. How the
minotaur

          poses like God
in his mystical cellar.

     Yet F. too brings the good news
that deciphers time
in focus, traveled by a map,
          as if one could say
          there it is! now is as good
               as anywhere.
     Everything is abstract
          in its origin almost
               as if Plato
          believed in the verity
of his good republic.

The escalator goes flat by
          steps. It continues
          as breath does:
               two men in blue suits with vests.
     The moving sidewalk is
               no less.
It slows into watchword, and if F.
          abhorred the occult,
          Jung compared sexuality
     in the psychic order
to a hidden grammar,
          dogma on the harpsichord.

          Organized
     mystery, lens-defined
          hyperbole.
A science rises from obsession,

shaped like the Golem of Prague,
but who remembers
          his song?
          Jung catches flies
            instead of fish.
F. hangs his briefs
          on the line.
              The world is all
                alone,
          all there is
          to imitate.
Time limps behind
the escalator, F. stands
          with a stopwatch,
      Jung with a camera.
Mind in slow motion, caught in breath.

Tall World

Melancholia.
The heart flaps its wings, but
doesn't rise.
It's the end of psychiatry if
90 percent of impotence
and frigidity is organic.
Sadness infects
opportunity. The boy on the
shoulder
complains of indecent proposals, but
will not grow into them.

It's a tall world in which
humor stagnates and someone like
Homer gets lost in translation,
although
he sees enough
to drive himself back
to Greece.

How does your analyst talk about
his wife/her
husband?
The face in rictus
can't discuss
how it fed
music through its teeth.

The boy became
a painter

of red surrealism. He met
Rimbaud in exile,
corrupted by art and madness.
Still boys,
still arriving from the country.
The boy, unnamed, described his life
as winter in the seed. He clanged
against his future as a businessman.

He felt better
when he changed his name,
author of sexual voices
as he heard them
on a drunken racing yacht.

Confused by thought,
the brain clutches itself
like a crab.
If the organ is impotent,
whose talking cure
will halt at that moment?
Think of your house
under centuries.
Passion is enough
to paint in red cloves,
a burdened
table.
But no insurance
is better.

When will day
cling to the brain-figures
of night?

The man suggests a lesion, or
did he mean a legion? Running
                    guns
                    too fast.
          Life
        has no insurance.
Doctor Gachet leans his head
      against the air.
          Van Gogh noticed
                a fly
          in his mantra.

Doctor Jung collected
                    conscience,
        as if to splice events
        into a caricature of the human.
          Even so, no image
                was enough.

    No use following the man
beyond the stages
of success in the billions.
Secretly, he had always hidden
          a Derringer in his
                mind.

He died like a lamppost
                standing up,
        lit by a blue light,
      hazy under the drifting stars.

Bad Dream and the Friend

I

At the corner of war and money,
the curtain opens a supposition
        that age
               will go
      gently enough.
    Civilization rubs us
            the wrong way.
    If only we can
be happy for a brief time,
      like all happiness,
    our minds
clear,
the weather blue
      as in childhood.
    The muse would not
              terrorize
      us
    as the past does.

I dreamt of war: the Nazi doctors
    in the camps,
        treating
their patients to death.
        And I
        in it,
an American soldier, a hollow contour.
      One of them

threw a hand grenade,
and my head
        exploded.
    I woke
with the book I was reading
        in my head
                like an echo
                of that time.
    My son said:
                    so stop
reading that book.
A dream of annihilation
        wishes for
        such instruction.

II

        This critical friend
is in a condition,
                blood
        seeping
from his guts. He recurs
    like the full moon,
            red
        in his heart,
going out, waning forever
He dreamt
                perfectly:
        versions of tradition

in song and ballad, and of
> the moment too:
political in his roaring salt.

Going, the ephemeral, the phone bills,
> liberation as
>> a mode
> of conquest.
Going, the roof,
> the cupid.
> Gone those early days
> harbored in forgetful mind.
> Gone, a woman,
Elizabeth, red hair
> glinting in lamplight.
The jeweller fits
> diamonds into our eyes'
>> setting.
A pear falls. The friend's
> heart goes out:
> red, frying.

Surreal Love Life

Someone who appeared,
    head leveled, a disgrace
for public relations, determined
a woman as centerpiece
to the domination of owls. Each sweet
        sway
    encourages designation
      as the favored wineshop.
    Entropy in clusters
    figures in F.'s calculation:
  the swim of soup
in the mind's cadaver.

One can go from stutter
        to cadence
and call it a theory
      of accidentals.
F.'s thought winks
    at his fellow
      headblazers.
Why did Freud brood except to please
  his young lovers, who
slept
    in the cellars?
Beyond which there is no
      wife
  older than she can be.

Yet if F. loved
no one could recognize it

in the sexual attitudes
        of his blue papers.
He troubled the air
        by breathing it
        so dominantly.
            When the story
                runs out,
        the white-fingered Lord
assumes a special value,
a stalled hypothesis, as if F.
        dreamt in colors.

        The situation retires
        for the night. Martha's sister
is thought to be the woman who
                leaked
                into F.'s mouth.
        One attempt
        is never enough to secure
                the cherry trees.
F. is not unknown to love,
but is old enough to drive
        a strong suspicion.

The surrealists, of course, veered
        into his headlights
        like frigid antelopes.
            They oiled the unconscious,
                crossed
        themselves with red hearts.
They believed in transcendence
        as the name of words.

F. was a man of connections,
a tiger leaping into
          sunflowers.

Success doomed them all.
The French stood in line:
          Breton, Desnos, Eluard.
Breezes cooled the hot
          pastry shops of
               Vienna.
Stravinsky. Picasso.
          Nijinsky.
None of them ever died, so suddenly
did the world around them empty.
Freud, in his pajamas, still waits
          in the vestibule
                    to greet
Mother Night with questions
and surprising, incurable answers.

A Trickle of Flame

Took the winter gun
as token of independence. Of
someone
to mail to,
accident of occasion
when the wall turned blue.
For a change, I don't think
of F.
but of how crisp the firmament
is today,
as in the picture-book of childhood
before the onions
sliced my time
in half.

I read that the ideas
are available, but put together
with bad correction:
a flutter of
wallpaper.
F. returns in organization, a tilt
in key. I order him
like breakfast.
The faucet releases dimes
in the marketplace.
Very well then, he was a chain
of command. He was good
like toast.

I saw a trickle of flame cross
        my lover's eyes, otherwise
        black like salt.
    But she had said *assault*, something
salmon in the skillet. Could he
                help me?
        The correspondence was technical,
        a ghost in the factory
    where ideas
were turned out much like
                indignant water.

    The door handle broke
as I turned
                it
        to my left,
        away from trouble.
    F. spoke
in my thought in Tom McGrath's
                voice,
        my teacher
when I was young and still believed in
                tuxedos.

The girl had a blue necklace
    tattooed around her neck.
    What weariness of pain
    can break us all! As when
                F.
        declaims in the amphitheater
        outside Greece
    an organic analysis

that I can feel
unburdens my love, rusting in the
                    years.

    Parts of speech do not help.
Water is too gray. Particular episodes
grind in the brain.
The Carmelites leave their winter
                quarters.
        The sea is pure fish.
        Why didn't I choose Jung
who contains a charm of symbols?
        If I question
it is because I believe
        my teacher's poetry lives
                starkly,
            without attenuation.

    The picture-book of childhood
assumes less importance as I move
toward my shadows in the brain.
        Yet there is reason
                to predict
            a sun in silence.
    I have murmured the name
until its flesh has peeled away
            and the bones dried
        in valediction.
    Home is where my lover lies
                open,
            eyes of flame.
We wait only for thought's indulgence.

Our Group Back Then

It was 40 years ago:
    all the plums I imagined
    have not survived.
    We sat around
        in a contemporary
            way.
I said what I believed
    to be evidence
        in that case.

    Their focus on F.
    was not clear. Mine was
        hesitant.
Sometimes a roof
knocked on the door. Little lapses
        in suicide
        occurred.
The head guy sustained intervals.

    To be wrong
    turns out a simple
        syllogism. A way
            station
        away from
        whatever was said
in the beginning.
        Afterwards we went
            next door
    to the deli.

Whatever remained was eaten.
Yes, we staggered after truth.
    We lifted 10 times our weight
    How antlike our eyes,
              seeing
      their choice
of dimensions
like yesterday's salad.
Often we liked each other
as proof of similar ghosts
      in the bedroom.

      I confronted a woman,
    told her she was
              a gadfly,
poking around
      in the world's business
      but hardly touching mine,
          as I wanted.
We weren't supposed
to fraternize, yet I knew
love
            scurried about
      in temporary homes.

I was married, had found my limits
    of sexual wonder:
      sex as intruder, another.
Time skipped the senses
      as we talked
inside the clock, moved
            by hands
      we couldn't hold.

The pity of therapy
is its incandescence, fireflies
   that weave through each cranny
         of air
     only to lose in darkness
     the breath of knowledge
  in a gasp, a wheeze,
body's betrayal.

The mind maybe
         learned
that it's just the brain,
   acting out its cues, as it must,
      on a stage
     with dimmed footlights.
We slept while we talked: fond
       whispers
   we could barely hear
  through our dreams.
Later we went home separately
and considered how well
   a thought could end.

Professional Dreams
for Dr. Denise Farnath

I took the hand-pats as surety
for a purpose I could only dimly fathom.
       She brought me to
       a winter garden where I slept
in her professional dreams
          for several nights
       as we carried on
       the troubled healing.

To be the doctor at such times
when the chatter of a patient's illness
disturbs the rigor
          that is learned in memory,
         breaks open
     those closed passages
traveled alone. Patience accumulates
like withered limbs in the eyes
          that see
     deep into alternative roots.

I talked about first names, I who
          always hid
        my own.
I learned Greg's, Bob's, Andy's, also.
But what's in a name when the one-eyed man
      lolls on a lollipop, an old
         geezer
      with a mind to go back

into the bright imagination
of dawning light. Lick the dream,
            he thinks,
      before the moon comes
full circle on a stick, too sweet
to be denied its fulfillment, its dead
            seas.

What the doctor opens with her acuity
      may be nothing less than
      a whisper in the dark,
      from shade into glaring
                  distinction.
      I make out only shapes, blurred,
            thick as rocks.
I think like dry lemons, myself in memory,
a tune forgotten except as she
      hums her own echo.

      I am exhausted and sleep
      with a patch on the wrong eye.
            Later a horse will gallop
                  into my dreams,
                  a little loco,
      white-maned, as I am.

My doctor's professional outlook
is the eye I lack.
                  My own
                  names
            arrived starkly from
      their local anesthetic.

That was long ago, in mind,
before she became the monitor
        of my hazy meditations
concerning the letter E.
I look for vision to the language
        my surgeon
            knows.
        Who can I be
that I lose the words to describe
who I am, one-eyed? She tells me—
        I, the child
        of my greater age—
how to spell what I cannot see.

Yellow Stripe

As if it were the stripe
I follow, yellow. In my dream,
        the shade barely mentioned.
    But this was not the sun
            I followed.
A lunatic on the loose, a fragment
        of despair wherein
    the location
is solid. A dawn
somewhere in my passion.

    The others come after
            I push,
and the Congresswoman loves me, other
than the party. Belief
        holds a bouquet,
        without a budget.
I am left to her right, where the sun
            creeps in.

Another day I follow in my desire.
Time upsets what I can't see,
    the chauffeur dying at the wheel.

        My position
    is aligned with space too
            awkward
    to modernize. Certainly I come
bridgewise: a locus outside

the dream.
A priori, the poem
in all this
ended before I could
tell it.

The resin in my wound
is her idea of conduction,
which reveals a detractor.
I am not wise enough
to detect
the motive that campaigns
for her love. The train left
yesterday
and followed a single
track
whence so much woman
thought to be alliterative.

Too flash, I think,
stopping in the middle
of winter. The snow conducts
moderate illusion. When will
the asteroid come?
Shadow lurks,
stuck in similar
anchor.

The yellow line
is behind me, as I see in the
construction
of this dream:

man-made, artificial,
in which I hear
the raucous peacock scream.

Off-center, the bearer of zones.
Sex is the counterpart, what is not
dreamt of.

Syntax, left in the church,
provides. If I wake up
from language,
no one will know.
One whodunit
is just the next one, and Heather
will do me in like a felon
for love
of Washington.

Yesterday approaches
fresh as a clean window.
I stop and alight from the dream,
where I have been on the road
too long.
She takes my hand,
an appointment kept.
Applause. O, applesauce! One more
act
to go.
I forget my lines.

The X Factor

Jesus, many-sided messiah,
        not yet come,
        ever coming,
extends from the older prophets:
   Isaiah, Elijah,
     Jeremiah.
As a Jew, I drink a wild cup of
        red wine
       every day
for my health—the way has been long
    and restless. Overhead,
    a vulture lowers,
      ecstatic.
  I am incarnated as ego,
  id, libido, superego,
    as are all.
The day disguises the German-speaking
      master
     from his prey:
  jelly world, excellent blood,
taboo.

     Mind is a pilgrim,
footless but energetic. Nerve goes
before you can time its destination,
    and forever the hour stops
     at the childhood corner
    where God stood
in the intersection, dazed

by sheer imagination.
    Now Father Freud implicates
        a fixation
    as a dramatic mood in which
    the moon shadows alder and oak
in a romantic liturgy.
    Now is a good time
        to reflect
on the cloudy breath of his books,
when submerged in art and poetry.
Relatives rescued him from drowning.
    But in other cases,
      he visited with bouquets,
        departures.

Time to go home. The winter
   startles us,
      beseeching
as it does,
     beaching the whales,
       as it does.
Poetry continues,

       the doctor
listening to heart, lungs,
  which do not lie.
     Voice at the last
culminates in visionary
    silence.

Weighing the Balance

A certain lack
of balance
criticizes me,
my slack departure into
vagueness where I feel
my walk
slightly above the ground. What
causes this
is age and a loss of
clarity in choosing neighborhoods
outside my nodding voice.
In the movies
I am dark,
a motion among seats
occupied by sinister people
ready to throw me down.

Descent is more difficult than
rising in this new dust
that coats my lips, dries them
as meditation prefigures.
If I am dizzy in my self-analysis
of Freud
it is due to my
running eyes that
see temptation in words
as a form of courage. It's all
visual,
a vision bound to

corners of Plato, who
saw shadows where men were,
and perhaps showed in mind how ideal
the hourglass was,
based
on sand-pyramid
scales.

If I trip, serenity calms me.
Fallen into trust, I blink twice shortly,
a long look, my own Morse
to rescue.
When I change voice to a classier
villa
I think the philosophical republic
will welcome me as a liar.
Coda takes up what I left behind.
This winter
is slow in piling up snow.
No moisture
restricts how smoothly
the great doctor's wisdom
lies in shadows.
Fire answers the blankness of thought
when not filled with words
assigning understanding.

Spring's light lifts copious
signatures as if one moved
through the first question preserved
in stone.
Plato was not Freud's

favorite Greek, only
an idea frayed in transit.
Jocasta, mother loved in body by
her young
king,
knew little
of the temperature she wrought
in art's
science. She held me
when I was young and her son.

On my own, I catch glimpses
as I tread on, warily, afraid of
stairs,
longing to look clearly
at those younger years
shadowed in memory.
Was I ever healed by Freud's
dream-children?
Wearily, I am alone, my self
framed by wood-nymphs,
the woman I love screened
behind abstract principles.
I, prime character, mover
in all my fictions,
lean lightly into
the spring winds,
courting nature's first law, love's
scribe
tossing about in the balance.

X's and O's

They are teaching
footballplayers
manners:
how to eat with double forks,
how to drink sanitized punch, how to
say hello,
moving their lips without their
hands.
It is grueling to be exacting exactly
off the field where
corpses
lie buried,
so near to ancestors, those boys, tackling
one after another.

In another century, in Europe,
that would be a good day of atonement
for all those dropped passes, those
shapeless blocks. One
is never enough
to squeeze
the lover's hands,
to frame silence as a force
to seize the analyst by the throat. Those
days,
when hope was equal,
linger even into dotage as a thread
that leads away
from that ancient bull.

X's and O's are just
for those who sleep under bridges when
night comes
in judgment.
They too played
football
in their time
of increments and swollen
eyeballs.
Today there are women too,
rummaging in their hearts for one
last
cheer.
The analyst's job is to shatter the eggs
of the ego almost as well
as Dostoevsky, Kafka, and some other
interior linemen. Poems also
for the broken edges,
where the whites of their eyes
turn green.
As those barns that double
as cloisters
grow cool, memory-laden,
all those good times!

To sleep is to waken into darkness:
shadows of the sun, and
as the analyst
proposes,
the normal in brackets.
To list all the names
everyone shoulders against

all other names
would be erroneous, a fumble
in the end zone.
Recovery comes late for some:
even the analyst never gets too far
from her analysis.

The aim of God is often
unsure,
and so it is a sign
of indulgence to accept the analyst
as a part-time mentor,
not as a religious but as a connoisseur
of the sex trade. Let
the moment
slip away,
she urges: it is the wrong one,
it seduces with banal signals.
The idea is, wait till old age, aim
with a flabby
foot
for the center
of the goalposts, lie down
on the bench. The rest is quick
and to the point.

Ego Symbolizes

I am ridden
        to tears
by a squint in the map that colors
    F.'s early symbolism. Oedipus
smokes a crumpled cigar in the bar,
beard white as camphor balls. The father
reads a passage around the block
                three times
        as if to prove heartshaped love.
    The daughter conceals
rhythms that dry on the line.
    F. is causal: yesterday's
                hero.

    I suggest to myself
implausible virtues. Truth is
louder than words. Psychotherapy
                adjourns.
    F.'s science
has moved to another neighborhood.
        I am lost
        without his provocations,
        and regulate my sins
        with iron testicles.

He wrote of ego
    as the conscious misfit,
the white knight of uncharted
            regions.

I am lost
in Aztec civilization
with one extra
heart
for the executioner's knife.
F. taught me how to scream
after the canyon's echo.

Tomorrow is yesterday without a past:
a thought especially
effective
when I recognize symptoms
like dry mouth in New Mexico.
My death trots around me,
harbinger of rubber horses.
F. is a collaborator
in my life.

And yet someone said
Jung is more interesting. I think
this is because he collected more
symbols.
He said mother
and all the mothers
answered the call.
He and F.:
psyche's tectonic plates.
But F. is Godless, represses
the lachrymose syndrome.
He will not weep for
the hardening
of my blood. Jung cripples
my anxiety.

I am my process. I regard the night
    as a lost day, during
which I could dream within reverie,
      with the ego's help,
      though ego even so,
        would risk the
          the deep bogs.
  Who is God
that F.
     symbolizes Him?
  I, who am not
        a Symbolist,
    live in mystery, I,
    my own father.
This is an afternoon among others
when I read the sun's shadows
    that compose my image.
F. has moved out. He took his
       cigars,
    his clock,
and all his life savings.

Making Real

F. clings to the wings that
                    culture
    lets fly into thermodynamic
    levels otherwise subdued
    in women's arms. The man
        waits outside, limp
as noodles. Whatever chooses to abridge
            toward distraction
        is a feather in his eye.
    Especially the king's
                fool
        remarks the greasy
        ancestor. Honda Accord
demonstrates a material
                skill
        F. could discern
    as a fact compounded
    of social enterprise
in common with smooth
                capital.

Yet, tactfully, the maroon moon
    hangs in the sky
        as a woman hangs
    in the man's loop. Or dug
                into
    his lap. A vacation
attends what was there before
the action vacated. We spell our

name
with five zeroes,
as if to be in that zone
requires
rehearsed
amplitude. Or the woman dead,
surfaces
among killer whales.

But we don't get this
from F.
or his
acolytes, for at no time
is he more charming than when
he expostulates against well-tutored
women.
That he is dead
is a concept that recoils
in the mind,
springs loose among bodies.
The thought he conceives
realizes, makes real, what warriors
sang in Provence,
warblers like rain,
like passages.

What happens then is that
his case
gives us conceptual
accuracy if not always fact.
Weapons are an index
of simple blood-smart. They flow

across pages, warping sound.
A woman hopes for
visitors, likely as angels,
genderless,
former spooks.

F. takes us in confidence that we too
reside on Arcturus,
purple as in a child's astronomy.
What we do must identify
combinations of genes that
fabulate our motions
on blankets
on the park
grass.
When all is said, nothing remains
but hierarchy.
Time swivels
on its loop.
A creaking chair points to
a complexion of austerity.
We think Bartleby
is such a man.

Then there is a combination
safer than what we
imagined
or F. pointed out
in advising adjustments
to invigorate principles.
He was the man who, in part,
corrected the century.

Yet
he could not make
a science of repressed
awakenings. He could not
repeat
the mother in the son nor
extrapolate sin from the unconscious.
He revealed in the sense of
a poet
in good prose.

It is easier to live
among people divined
from animal guts than
ephebes
marching in jungles.
Where does luck exist
before it shows its black ink?
A fact, then,
in the avant garde,
though F.
saw such faces half in shadow,
the other half in growth.
He may have believed better
of his enterprise
than his words occasion.
I, for one, still intuit
the velocity of his truth.
The lion
stretches,
growls softly
into the microphone.

Freud in California

California dried up in me,
    the song stopped
    on a note. What was rendered
deserved no description,
    The group met
    late afternoons. The weather
    grew hair.
    Freud spawned
the surrealists, who slept
with their eyes open. Ordinarily,
    someone
    would quote
    only part of the sentence.
    Ordinarily, we would go home
after more talk. No one knew
    the world
    after it was fried in oil.
    Vastly concurrent.
    My thought slept
    in the snow
    that I imagined.

Suggestively, the group described
a general portrait of someone nobody
    knew,
    California was at stake.
    It was wise
to have moved the continent
    westward.

The threat
posed in the window,
the feeling of being
elsewhere, approached by naked women.
Forcefully, I clung to a root,
below me
the rushing water
of a tear.

How far can we go
in illustrating avid influences?
As a group, we were fishy, demanding
the cure
by eloquence.
One night I dreamt of Freud with onions
but would have preferred him
with macaroni.
It never rained
while we were shining.
But what were
the problems? How intellectual
might Picasso women be?
There were witnesses inside the radiance:
the black moon of stars. I told her
I could do some of that,
the figure in the patch.

We talked it over. Painted selves
in a coffee shop next to
the building.
Whatever the angle, I could see
into

their vague descriptions.
When I left California
I was worried *news*.
Therapy remained in the back of my mind,
suddenly gregarious,
a weight I could stagger.
The reason was distinct:
olives in the oatmeal.

The Women

From somewhere
the words describe the silence,
          coming from noise,
          from Cage's runaway
                    notations.
     Once the truth came from baby wails
like a passenger on a red-&-green
                    trolley.
     We don't hear
cameras any more either. The cop
          stands with his tired
                    pistol,
               without guile,
a filled motion of vacancy.

     When Freud came along,
some women trusted in his future,
          thinking they too
        needed a penis.
     Envy, he told them,
                    the canary's
                    tweeting.
     As if they were maligned
by nature,
                    returned to noise,
          the sweet of heart
          raged like peacocks,
or diverted words: more subtle peahens.

Jealousy,
he said, fears
the dark. Children thought
in measures
of uniforms, police. The one
on the corner walks
from evening lamplight into
groaning alleys.
Polymorphous is not
perverse, as the guru imagined.
Cage's precision is the waking
of random forces,
as the I Ching projects.
And children read omens
like miniature prophets.

Ozone protects Earth's blue
marble
some of us play with
at the speed of art.
Great master,
tell us now from your secret
files why women
say so breathlessly what wisdom admires.
Castration is the middle term
of the trinity that shapes
perhaps conciliation
between
male rhyme
and female's tender obituary.
No use explaining:
Earth consumes its own gravity.

The aleatory rises
from the level plain.

Dear daughter of my sometime energy,
how I played in your contemplation
as when I wished for any dream
            you could give me
        to change my way,
                put me among
        the high ancestors, the deep
                    originals.
I praise the eloquence
            of chance
        that thinks for me
as I dream. I move
                to Freud's
other goodness, his dazzling eye
        in mind's microscope.
Women are not his vision of genius:
        they are too jealous.
    He worked backward
    from logic to vulva.
I see in my daughter that marathon nature
that passes by the clever horseman.

This Might Have Been a Case

F., when he waited
for lab results, was
the middle man between candor
and transcendence. What if the
patient
betrayed his illusions?
His field
was round as a marble,
sperm encased in glass.
Atlas
in consequence.
A young woman, call her
Lili.
So much case in her mind.
Weary of compulsive influence:
a radio,
old Emerson,
Little Orphan Annie.
There is a time gap.

The results were conspicuous
like the gold watch
F. wore with its gold chain
in his
vest pocket, always the arranged
hour.
She thought in poems,
she bruised her eyes
on words.

The rabbi
had enrolled her between God
and the medicine cabinet.

Did F. lust for Lili? Did he even
know her?
She is not a case he mentions
among the early devils
of his breed.

One thinks of F. as a
peninsula
riding high in muddy waters.
His voice
had cancer, too.
He wasted the perfect broom
the burghers of Delft
had bestowed on him
in a Vermeer painting,
now lost.
Frequently, he polished his boots
during the casual rites
of summer.

A bleeding mind suggests
the independent choir that still
sings
after thought's
date
has expired.
F. sometimes worked a case
backwards

as in saying and so forth before
                external
                sources
        had been cultivated.

This Lili was not of his devising,
        but her case was always
                opening out.
Vienna's mayor, handsome Karl Lueger,
                an anti-
                Semite,
        escorted Lili
    back and forth,
    although she was only a name.

    Theory is sometimes more
than paper, as wind
is more than air. F. did not
                write
        abstractly. His cases
    were dignified, dressed properly
        and passed with
                the speed of
                life.

The rabbi lingered
        in Lili's breath,
                sweet wine,
        Old Testament
        cramps in her legs.
Mercy
    came to her,

flying over the rooftops dressed
like a bride.
She vanished from her own
imagination
when F., a future still in mind,
fled Austria to drift away
among London's shops and
bobbies.

A Question of Dogs

My mind in disjunctive order, its
            white stripes
            and black stripes
      cancel whatever halts
         in the road
         without reason.
Zebras in phalanx, I, like a judge,
     scanning interludes. Is the sun
             Jewish?
       Maybe. As I
       used to ask Ma, is that dog
             Jewish?
That depends on its owner,
          she always said.

Even then I blushed to think of a woman
on the table, thinking of questions,
    civil disorder in the single
           bathroom.
    I think of passion
        as tea or biscuits in the Tate
           Museum.
Freud in England,
dying of poison in the jaw.
This when I was older and devout
    in prayers I didn't understand.
        Meanwhile, where did that woman go?

       I talked myself

out of the cure. Adherence
to a tin code
is like never knowing, why
                Orphan Annie?
When God talked to me then,
                I thought
                it was
my meager knowledge of Freud.
Truth, a balancing act, and I
                a touch of
                    vertigo.

    I plan beyond
    the worried flowers.
        Something spooky
    in a glowing red watch. I see
time
going so fast
        my eyes can't keep up.
                Morning
    and the bamboo poles
hurt the rain. I remember the
                    woman,
        a chocolate shake
        right in the middle.

    Who foresaw the danger
I lapsed into in the distance
louder than wakefulness? It wasn't
            a dream,
        I'm sure.
I'm tired of dreams,

mentioning them like a list.
I'm not any better than I was before,
            confessing
                my first kiss.
        I feel like a
                    parallelogram.
                my rooms tilting.

Enough, I think. If I could have
                met Freud,
            what a fellowship!
        what spirit in the flies
            buzzing on the windowpane.
    A long service
predicated on small experience.
        Surely I can draw
                a good hand.

Water bubbling on the burners
detaches: balloons on the
                    ceiling.
            A sentence
            hovers in my back yard.

I surrender to words that move me
                around:
            bits of climax
                in the pudding.
End of the sentence completes the edge.
I ride a zebra and fall into anguish.
Freud again hangs by my hair,
            not much now that I'm old.

Composite in Black and Blood

for Mary Rising Higgins

Black man
   sleeps in his own
        blood,
     a taxi
     pulls away.
He was holding his baby,
a shoulder given to affluence;
his wife maybe
      was she tan only
        in that light?
           A famous
literary figure who—
what about that MacArthur?
     He came to read on campus,
     sleeping then through
        his own blood.
        She is tan,
    maybe black.
   Outside, the leaves
shine, but he was nice to me
        before that,
    before the fake shot
    pushed his blood out.
No reason
to be shouted in the blue
        atmosphere,
     in the worried
    black's calling.

The word is less than mourning
compared to his frozen shoulder
where the baby was still
        as ice itself.
        The other woman
                smiled,
                I think,
                at me.
Definitely white,
and I was unwise to the way
        we protracted the range
of his sudden sullen witness.
The MacArthur fated the taxi
                pulling away,
        or did the wrinkles
in the black man's eyes
                harden the air?
He snored into his blood.
        The smiling woman
                verged on bliss,
                though only the fresh
                        snow
augmented the future.
        I slept in his blood
                while the baby
        organized a simple death
                in my cold temple.
The clock came suddenly
                out of the west.
        I didn't know how much
                longer
        I could draw

the water out of his heat.
Was it the fury of his name
that brought me to the door
        of his terrible
                look?
        His blood ran into
                the river
where the mountains ended.
Topographically, I could never
                complete
the index that molded
        my composure.
When he woke, the theory
                began.

Narrative of Conscience

A breeze blows through my worksheets
    at five o'clock, when the sun,
        in its decline,
        opens out
to the owl
    of the local universe. I have
           followed
           my feet
      through the turnstile
      of this time,
    last night's kitchen a dream
      where I strayed barefoot,
          crawling,
      not knowing
      this was a phase,
only excess of being.

Lithe forms of women slant my mind
to wayward afternoons
        when in youth
    I took purchase
      on punishment.
   There is always
too much to think of. How could
        anyone
     rise on the shoulders
   of reverie
to see down below a scarred winter?

     Freud was only
       a name

in the crackerjack box.
Later, he slept in me, I, crank
of masturbation,
early riser
to a girl's breath
in my mouth,
comrade to beasts, siphoned
from liquid books.
Writing is too narrow:
a world glimpsed as a formal
target.
I aimed low at Freud,
crawling on all fours,
under the table, wax
fruits upon it.

Old now, I read
poetry, and write
for my heart's flickering.
Old Yeats, be my darkness,
beam through me a glow
of your Byzantine
years.
If in language there could be
reward for lines
silent in meaning
yet above mere duty,
I would speak to Auden's
limestone.
Song, though old-fashioned,
remains the lodestar,

from back then when syntax
refused the noose.

The third millennium:
        before it dawns in 24
    circles, spaces already its
                numbers
through asteroids' perilous design.
I call for mother, too dead
to believe me. But then she was
            a bastion,
        protector of my childhood,
    adolescence, young manhood.
In my new age I try to wipe
her blue eyes from
                my fingers.
Freud, help me
            sing
        one or two of your great
        oneiric sex-songs.

    I sell my dreams now
for pennies by the pound.
            It's not too late
        to believe
            in Jung's
    collective irony. I too
am a myth, as described in prologues.
Walking the labyrinth is an ancient
                spiritual
                exercise.

I have walked it
on filmy shoes to scan
        its negative. My penis
            wakes up.
I think it wants to shout.

I might have been a Language poet,
        but of course
my tongue is too long.
        Instead, I
            respect
those who crack each word
with a mallet until it cries
            with joy.
I am the narrative
of my conscience: I hold the hand
        of strong masters.
I am pitch black, though
a light swivels through my head.
        Yes, old fellow, I talk to myself
            in brackets.
The main story idles
        in lemon-light.
Nowhere to go but here,
where I eat oatmeal, mango, Cornish hen,
        and pull along the shy God
of my heirs.

This Caption for Life

He is young, just out of middle school
where he studied the gaps
          in his life
     as if this could teach him
                    the habitation
          of his days.

He hears shots from across
          the border. But this is merely
               Exhibit A
          in the more likely definition
of a clinical study by white-suited
                    people.
               If he survives
          he will be cast in mythology
     as one who learned early
how to ride the mourner's
                    prayer like a horse.

This is a sentence. He is guilty of
          leading a private life.
     He never heard of Freud
     or any of his progeny.

     Time is left over
when he sleeps, his heart
blown away by many incidents.
          There is something
                    textbookish
     about his constellations.

He is his own persona,
embittered by the changeless
rotation of the Earth.

Failing at the birth of life,
Earth is weightless, harbinger
    of a more solid air, in which
    even Mars could breathe.
    Losses can be articulated
solely by good songs of a
    hand that reaches in stealth
        or the practice
that teaches the ordeal of
                gravity.

Yet, to earn patience
            is a mortal
                exercise,
    as though death could not
            matter
except to idealists. One hungry
            guard
    at a crepuscular outpost
can't justify a reason for
            therapy. The cure
        for his life
    exhausts itself
in the synchronized version
            of myth.
But Jung is too early for his mind.
    He will pace to and fro,
    shouldering his rifle,

until the wind
blows through his head
and he fires
at what is only a whisper
across the border.

He will not stay at his post forever,
he will be relieved, will return to
his village
a hero
for having survived
life in an average way, as it is
thought
by other harvesters
of all their dead
moments.
His face will be nurtured
in primitive newspapers,
in yearbooks of colored obituaries.

Controversy: The Beginning

He held this idea
   in his hands
      so that
   it wouldn't fly away
in the migration of bats. An idea,
someone might have told him, is
      a bird.
   Freud wrote like a muscle,
attuned to the mind's red rubber,
the stretch between golden
      sources.
   For a while he was
      X-rated
because his willingness to live
in the future overcame
what he owed to the past.

He once told a woman, injured
   in a car accident, to listen
      to Brahms.
   This was not a treatment
      he would later think to use
      in the unconscious wilderness
where sunlight shows through
      only as a gap
         among bones.
   Freud wrote in a dominant key
as others might occupy
      words as illusion.

For repression hinted at
a fish
in the bakery. Little could be
done
with zero sustenance,
anorexia of the soul,
although he used
language
like a pinball bouncing off
objections,
non-confessions.

Freud treated memory
with blue gloves
something to show his vision
after the hour was up. He reversed
views in mid-fall.
Sections broke off in the shallow
universe,
in the cradle.

Time results from loneliness,
the ego dipped in chocolate
to entice bronze statues
to follow
human feelings.
Freud wrote as someone repelled by
bloc parties, voters
consistently out of touch
with their own minds,
which are surreal.

He campaigned
for truth
in advertising
no matter how hard it is
to hear the listener.
When psychoanalysis became
commercial,
voices plugged up earlier
ears,
synapses split.
The mind slowed
to a drizzle.
To release the vacancy he beheld
in the social frame,
Freud
wrote
barely enough to sustain
his living in bourgeois dreams.

Diamond Tongue

With metalinguistic courage,
the voice puts on its lipstick. Femur
blessing, the as if of a fading hour
when the face breaks
its stumbling body.
The analyst intrudes
with a white
voice, to be charred in 50 minutes,
a precise value.

I had at first not understood
how the diamond could wait
that long,
the consequence so disguised.
I asked him how the mouth
could suffer so.
He avoided confrontation
by heaving a chair through the rose
window,
stained glass spraying
through the time
of intercession.

Afterwards, I would soak my mind
in saltwater
for an hour, or as long
as it took
to trespass
the fatuous intensity.
Somewhere, when the voice stops,
a culture breeds another science,

crammed into reading,
sight strewn about
        like a dead camera.
    If she wears the diamond
            in her tongue
        why discourage her,
    whose need
must be greater than mine?

In analysis, there is a quota
        of dubious propriety,
such as sextuplets asleep in the way
    the night moves toward
            France.
I speak to her with a tourniquet
        around my voice.
    The doctor's ears stiffen
in his rush
        to the bloodstained mountains.

Sex interrupts the tongue
        in the shoes
        of fluency.
The heart is incorruptible—
you know this without professional
            birdsong.
    I reverse my eyes. I think
        I was founded
    like a company. In the east,
she is strumming lightly no matter
        the noisy rain. I hear
        only the checkmarks.
    When I leave, laughter

precedes me, and I try to
            catch up.
    What is left
       is a sticky analysis,
      a voice without
resonance. My friend's expertise
follows me in the rearview mirror.
    I am safe in her sound
      despite my analyst's assurance
        that I am not well,
that I love what displaces me.

    The birds
on their high wire begin
       the morning
       like chirping targets.
The day will be assured and costly.
   Some zero-man will pay
   for the Earth to rent
a new inner
         space,
    yet there are enough words
    for all of us.
Dusk will come, darkening
    the shadows. The brain's
      ocean
will go on until its metallic
insistence at last ceases,
    when the night falls into
    its diet of wandering sleep.

Late Judgments

As F. would think of it, the wound
fills the mind. The mind, in its swarm,
    fills the body,
        bloody
in affection. Similarly,
an index coerces odd gods into
      a mix
of old words and new meanings.
    The lamp:
oil in a vessel, wick lit,
mentioned among the heavenly
        bodies.
Lamp light—the avenues new
    in the evenings when the mind's wound
    electrifies its patience.
      F.'s skull a flame
in the night watchman's lantern.

    F. watches the world
    accommodate its last judgment
murmuring defiance as it goes.
But he is too early to be an ending
    no matter who
        defiles him
with his own wound, printed
    in valedictory books.
He is among the chopsticks
      of science,
    whose head rested

on his mother's pillow.
He could not finish his
dream.

Bounded by the still emergency,
the crowd
spills over, spills
like beer-foam.
It will lose its
head. F. speaks
to the curtain
as if Polonius, struck,
would bring it down. Then a beer
in Vienna, a Jew-baiting city left over
from the Hitler war.
But F. was a stranger in the
Kingdom islands.
He regarded his final papers as a wizening
assignment.

Words listen to each other.
This is the mystery
of the world's synonyms,
of reason without
a hat.
Somehow, when the words are there
when you need them,
the memory's riches
avenge the drought
that often afflicts
the watery eyes of an old man.

He sits in his office
with a client, also a refugee.
They talk about history
        before the bombs
        would fall on England.
It is the wound's future, a barrier
            whose life leaks
        as destiny wills.
    But then to be a doctor
    dozing while merciless enemies'
            laughter
        becomes new with
                plunder,
            slandering.
F. dreams like a bear in a winter
of resurgence, before the fresh mind
            of spring.
    To die
is the last emergency:
    cows still give milk, horses
    gallop into the shadows,
            boulders dry up.

Freud Inquiry

In thinking a poem of Freud:
I'm slightly afraid the warm weather
may stop.
Dictionaries pronounce
only what is explicit.
The human mind can be articulate
despite its thought.
The warm flowers
dispute the bees.
More becomes less likely
in a Freud poem. A tricky
customer, so I
think in advance
of what could be rued
in isolation.
I will observe in meditation
his approach to women
who repress incest
as a matter, of course,
in blind Oedipus.

In his practice, Freud consumed
freethinking organisms
to reach a tighter pulse than could be
broomed in comprehension.
But he darted out, camouflaged,
from mind's thickets, swarmed in fact
through dead lines—
if I write them that way
and miss.

That was then in Vienna.
I think Freud was right
                in assuming
            his patients
        were obsessively bred
on wine and chocolates. His truths
are not scientific in the way
        a wristwatch is:
        take rather a fact
        of disposition and stretch it
        far and closer
            in recognition
                    of sex
                    in psyche
as irony, dumbstruck as
                    a child's
        lantern in the dark
night of egoistic calm.

Portraits of the dead hang
            in sleep's gallery.
They must be called to answer
        for living their own lives
            parallel to death, which is
        to some degree
a triangle. Two lovers and their myth.
Orgasm is a tonic to be swallowed
                in one gulp.
        Freud's is a casebook
not to be opened until I have read
                the glossary
        that accompanies
his passage through Jung's apostasy.

Including Sex

He worked to keep his mind
        unembarrassed.
He failed to repress
the Jew by cutting off
    a syllable:
Sigismund. Yet he was a Hebrew
even if Moses was Egyptian. Freud
    was stark as a skeleton
  in Hitler's eye, even though
the time had not yet come.

    To be repressed
      is kindling wood
        set to the burn.
Dusk waters the eye
  of what we thought
      was civilization.
  I would have talked
    to Freud
  in Vienna if I'd had anything
    to say
except that I was a woman
with a penis. Not homosexual
  but a wonder in my own mind.
  I convinced my
    manhood
even while Europe killed itself.

  What is personal
crowded Freud's mind like schoolboys

going home,
flinging themselves
            at the clock
that martyrs them all, dull,
      eyeless in Gaza, even if they see
         well enough to stumble
                  through walls,
through daylight
         when the sun
                  turns around
            to its black side.

   Then Freud was master
in somebody else's house. Virgins
               grew
      in the wisteria.
Their husbands flew in and out
of windows, leaving
            tickets
for Tel Aviv, for Islamabad,
for Rome, Shanghai.
         Already the drill drives through
      these sexual children;
            the girls boys know
quicken their stride. Who will be
                  lucky?
Or is that too emptied out, birdy omens
            going nowhere?

Depression

That Jewish kid with the Brillo pad
    in his hair
feels like myself before
       I learned to speak
           English.
    I visited
     a therapist
once a week. She listened
      to my stories
and prescribed a walk around
         the block
      every day.
  She spoke German,
but flexibly.

    I was depressed
   like a dead horse.
   Paul had gotten married
    some days before.
I was so anxious that
       the wedding
go well
that I walked in wet cement
for weeks until I got stuck
   and lost my shoes.
     They kept on walking
     through my head
     like military boots.

    But speaking English
was secondary

when I struggled onward
toward my 13th birthday.
All that youth
a mistake. I was old
already
in the wet year of the monkeys.
I breathed through asthma:
walrus
of wheeze.
Dr. K. later told me
she had almost hospitalized me
for asthma of the brain.

I penalize myself
for walking too slowly,
not keeping up. My knees
are bottle-caps,
my feet, sponges.
My wife walks behind me,
dead.
The world is my poltergeist:
a leprosy
of the soul,
my infinitesimal share of
the universal
embrace,
though as yet undetected
in the slides.
Dr. K.: Goodbye. You were a kind
patient.
And you, though younger, were

a motherly
archetype.
I'm on my own again, on American
tiptoes,
waiting to be kissed.

Dramatizing

It is said that the dream
dramatizes
              an idea.
Stubble in the wound, and a gray
    visitor hovers above
    hallucination. The ends do not
                cohere
          to form a loop.
      Gray eyes predispose.
The lieutenant colonel stands off
                wiser
    from his youthful background
in homosexuality. This was the dream:
          lion covering
                ground
        toward the kill
        of a dangerous man.
                    Hemingway?
      I aim, hit
a domino. All fall backward
        in one long, curving
                sweep.

Yet we spin our eyes, blurs,
    academic resistance.
    Who would relive the idea
    of a hand groping for the
                heart?
The kill is a kind of resurrection,
pulpy heartbeat. Interpreting figs

is the last resort
of a waning mind.
Waking, the moon low
in the morning light.

The first resort is a spa
in central Germany. I swim, draw
21
nine times in a row.
A man I don't know
suggests I cancel the dining room,
instead go naked
to his wife, who, he
assures me,
waits for me.
I wake up in her arms, forlorn,
blue flashes
going off in powder,
maybe rat poison.

I can no longer
ask
who the strange man is:
he is I.
Jung would say I am the archetype
of the hermit, in love
with my disgust.
This is a reckless view
of Narcissus, the pool of my eyes
lonely, seeking only
itself.
By my wife's ashes

I occlude
all sexual syntax.

Blue is the dominant
color
of patience.
The dream records instances
when God was alone with His
beast.
Already the locusts
swarm over the belly
of the dead man.
A crisis flies up
from the shades. No one
can leave through the wall.

I age again, hairy like a water
buffalo
standing in its own
shit.
Time drifts, unchecked by sudden
stops.
I bite into a pear,
lie down in the stinking grass.
I imagine a world like
any other,
and embrace the body,
hold it in my arms,
afraid it will tilt down
into the hardening milk.

One page after another
rolls off the copier,
green after red after green,
a book
with sound acoustics.
The eye glows in the city's
blackout
when all lust
curves into fast legs. The stranger
speaks
in the words of a stranger,
how he says
to the woman: don't be frightened
if I hold your hand. A moment
later
the fog swallows them. The plastic
canary
fills with steam
from a Japanese teapot.

Make It Orgazmic

The round ego
sounds with spherical egg
in mutilation
of series.
The therapist claims that
social dysfunction
is a private matter, shyness
the fate of young Jews.
The therapist catches innuendo
by the beard
as if
to chop it off.
Jung never met Pound
but they were
symmetrical.

Next we learn to liken image
to a recurring afflatus.
The bridge
is conjunctive
to discussion.
White flowers remain
in the discourse.
Eventually,
the ego splatters
on the frying pan. White rose
occludes.
Make it orgazmic, Ez
says.

Jung says that everything
happens at the same time.

Dead nuclear fuel transported
to the WIPP site near nuclear
libido,
source of neutrino
nightmares.
Gray rub of dusk
compromises time implication
where redwoods grow
what the therapist
forgets.
Mules on their feet,
forgoing incident
in the quiet yards.
Miles of redemption.
Jung years.
Ez much too stylized, too
damp.

We could live in the frat house
if we could somewhere
steal
a den father.
Water is the x factor
behind the junipers in our gardens.
Who are we?
We are wet,
our eyes drip shadows.
None of this is beautiful,
if one accords

language a part
in fate.
Jung analyzes Pound
by letter, finds no subject,
no one who fits the collective
murder in the park.

Let it rest in nature like a pious
bear
on all fours,
looking for a cabbage.
The light at Yellowstone
crawls farther away from
its limits.
The little girl offers the bear
a banana. It is shot
on the spot.
Pound wuz at St. Elizabeth's 13 years,
too proud to feign sanity.
Jung, in Switzerland, on his knees,
in his cage,
prayed to a marginal myth.

Thoughts, Loving It

How does something sound
　　　inappropriate
　　　　　to its cause?
　　　Love is power,
the engagement.
Stiff seabreezes dominate
　　　　　the mind,
wafted along
　　so much the incident
　　of its termination.
The process is like using the hands
　　　　　to mold
　　　　　words.

　　Psychology begins at home,
　　　what you practice,
　　the praxis of it.
If the father was pitiful, now to speak it
with judgment on the edges.
　　　　Mother, too
　　　repeats phrases
　　that depict her sad
　　　　　inheritance.

　　The body
must be a friend sculpting
　　　　　reason,
　　　not rising from a departed lover,
but in testament to what is right

about confusion.
To keep in mind
is inevitably the test, a tact
enacted
in daily reply to self's dogma.
Rich is the dialogue
between synapses.

Owning psychology becomes helpless
in thought. To pay for
critical information
one uses words like children's
blocks.
Anyone as icon
becomes vain as once the troubadours
wrote poems to their paramours;
loved and loving
as they thought.
What came of all that
is no more than a technical description.
Don Quixote.

When plastic night enters,
psychology develops the film
of daily usage. Here is sculpture
as bottom line,
marble in its rage.
Reason runs throughout,
pursued
by the Furies, predators
let loose from psychology who later
follow those horses

left over from movies.
    What is this but complexity,
        or possibly
            the other:
    man of woman's idea
of green, the motion of green,
like a huge worm shadowed by forest
    where the foot is blind.
    To avoid allegory,
the hands shape words in curatorial
        order,
    sometimes reaching
all the way to humankind.
    Waking up is serious. It brutalizes
    dawn/ dusk / dream,
    body already wild with arrivals,
      with place to spread,
      with feelings
    to believe.

Of Rats and Men

I

It scurries like a rat
in a series of loops, such
                    feeling
        that cannot hold
    its monstrosity
in check.
            The mind moves in lament
                for a yellow slicker
                    in the rain.
            To say it is his other
                        personality
        leaves out of account
who the woman is
        he could not leave
                    alone.
            But no matter:
        the trace is cold.

He opens his genitals to the wind
as if this was a force to make
            his prophecies true.
        Under analysis,
he grew foolish
            like cloth of gold,
            old-fashioned conquerors,
barnyard cock-a-doodles.
Not observed in the best literature,

he lost his lady
to the stars, glaring
like bad light bulbs
to the naked eye.

He is more of a basic action
than his name would qualify.
To disguise his reasons
would fail his case.
Yet philosophy must be
technical, otherwise
the love goddess
must confess to the
academy
her sins.
The rattlesnake
appears
in the driveway
emerging from what is left
of the unconscious
like a piece
of someone's body matter,
still writhing.

II

They called him Rat Man.
His rat was a penis aimed
at his father who,
though dead,

lived in Ernst's hidden copy
of the mind's extremities. Good Ernst
        masturbated
        like a housefly
    rubbing up
against the window screen.
        In the Orient,
they used to unload a bucket of rats
onto the criminal's backside
    and watched
while the rats chewed up
                his anus.
Ernst felt a regular, sidereal anger
        crumpled up inside
    his legal briefs.
A worm also weaseled through
        his nocturnal credibility.
Love aroused him to silence
        until his fingerprints
        were finally
        whited out
    in the Great War.

Irony Apropos

F., the square waltz,
forgathers what could only be
      torments, beginning glide
        squeezed from
          moths.
Feeble the light that squanders passion
    in dark stages.
     That woman who reminded you
      of what child
      you'd left foundering
      in chocolate milk
returns as your wife's maid.

    For all that
   you made it to an elite
of self-examination.
Only the sexual survives as an interlude
       between
       black-hatted
           gentlemen
   and buskins at ground level.
   Altogether a fix of
    muse-imbibing:
poets on parade.

And after 10 what number slides
     through mud
    to graze an assemblage
true to its word in hundreds?

F., the grass
is red
where you have stood or lain,
father of dreams, warrior in
galloping
trousers.

We wake along your path
who can no longer lie in your
memory.
To bring Easter eggs
to starving America was not
your sole motive.
Only you
record
the long-term patience to hold
against those who threw
stones at your mind,
and still believe in attacking
your ghostly-thick
eminence.

Women,
who might have
saved you,
recur in evening wine,
fist of semblance.
All has worked as a bromide
in the darkening drink.
You are now
the liar of Hamelin
by the court of so many lemmings

floating amid kelp.
Justice is not so neat
    as a composite biography.

Your progeny live in dried-out
              wind.
    Lucian Freud paints
    thick-veined legs, big bellies, fat
            jowls.
    Esther Freud writes about
         Glasgow
      some fictional German property
      west of love.
Who else follows you now in that family,
    devoted, perhaps misunderstanding?

      So it goes, human
      affairs in groaning corners,
sometimes the wit
    to leave alone
    flamboyant objects by conflict
         despoiled.
But then F., you were a Viennese
and wore the mind's medals
    on a camouflaged lapel.
    So much dense gloss
    to be faced
in dangerous couch-rooms.
The night-woman, slow in her age,
    cleans up
the debris.

London,
your last conversational office,
        where your mouth
            died
even while your memory stalked
thin Jewish women in red hats.
        Are you still talking,
            taking the cure wherever
        the sky fails?
Moments ago I saw you, F.,
        in my frame of mind,
            bearing a logic
to memorialize your art
with its scientific urge.
Only its beauty is true.

        I can't repeat you.
No one else can say the words you
                wrote
        with infallible accuracy.
        Neither yours nor Jung's
        chthonian world,
hidden side of Earth, which only
                the moon
                can face.
        We justly wonder
at the news you brought us
a century ago:
        lacking proof.

Traces

I have already done
　　　　the thinking
as sharp vectors
　　engage the thought, which is responsible
　　　　for the victim, who dies
　　　　　　in wait
　　　　beyond the snow.
This act of experience nurtures the various
　　　　　　genes
　　　that can't not experience
　　what they do
　　　or are done to.

Take that which
controls the tongue or lets it flap
　　　　　uselessly:
I choose a certain comfort to narrate
the time I spent walking in the small park
　　　behind my house
　　when a black terrier barked at me
　　　　　too closely
　　　and I couldn't grip
the quick emotion. I stood
　　　later, forgotten in the truth
　　of a prickly discomfort.

Nowhere could I resent
　　　the favor of my animal
　　　　　consciousness.

When I think
of my body
I am the self of the subject,
which I express as a plagiarist
of Hamlet,
his particular experience.
The sky is what dead poets called azure,
not a bad word
for romance,
although sheltering gifts
is also effectual. The sudden space between
two emotions can be sliced by two sharp
vectors,
differently acknowledged.
Yet if I think precisely
who would I know as an expression
of what is always left behind?

My first girlfriend would not dance
with a Negro,
not being a Negro herself.
She was brought up in southern Ohio where
elements of theory that weigh
the slavery of liberation
didn't exist
in several disguises.
She was otherwise modest and carried
a Derringer in her purse, having lived
mostly
among poor whites
near a hilly climb from Echo Park Lake.
I didn't know her Caucasian limits

until after the first flowering
had overflowed our dependence
        on what we associated with love.
Years afterward she visited me
    at my typewriter. Slightly overweight,
    she said, because her husband was elsewhere.
Bright in her talk she was, and I
    in my blush felt nothing
            but amity
        for such long remembrance.
Though my heart was theoretical
far beyond the snow that fell in many acres.
    She might be dead by now,
        I tell myself.
Regardless of Cupid's broken arrow,
    I burn incense, pitying myself.

    I think back
because it is harder to think forward,
the future besotted as it is by emanations
        not grounded in fact.
    That's the "always suppose"
            of nature,
        of human predilection
        as forgotten news:
        even the past a brown alley.

Thinking that I am done, I don't think.
Vanished faces tie up the phrasing network,
            in which I praise
        sun and showers that passed long ago,
            before I could name

who I was to be.
The quintessential is forever out of phase
        like an illness
           in the word.
      But I think of some rare beast
that runs to ground the victim,
        swift in her death,
          and thinking this
I too lodge in the eyes of myth.

Twisting Plane

Wear down gradually, granite
dry, dust cooperates, the hurricane
eyes
the shore.
Time to think about
such quality in the moon,
wolf waylaid.
Time gutted, an instinct.
F. stands,
a cactus
plant
in a red, chinked bowl.
Who misgives is a gift from
Gertrude.

But speech is
a physical act in the mind,
F. always elegant
on the cusp of disorder.
Six sides like a dead fish.
And he worries
afterward a context word
lacks.
Bees
stuff the air, vicious,
says Gertrude.

F. thought of scallops:
undersea equation. When

                    the Marx
                    Brothers
              arrived in Leningrad,
                  they ate herring
                          in Lubyanka,
        charged with disrupting the humor
              of collective farms.
                    F.'s world
        goes on
        without him, mildly conspicuous
              in all the wasted dreams
                      of human discontent

              His wife grows flowers
                      in his hair. You're
                      the perfect wife
        when he thought of her sister.
                  Beauty sought under
                  skin's paste,
                  but she loved thinking
        his thoughts,
                          vacations
              in the Alps, a noble drone
                  in his masculine hive.
        She wasn't attractive enough to find
              another man.

              Dream: at a table
              in Mannie's restaurant,
        sitting in a wheelchair
        where waitresses pushed him
                  toward a table,

the wheels resisting,
the cashier
watching.
Whose dream, Gertrude
inquires,
as she is awarded a lush painting
by Medicare?

I dreamt I was Freud afraid,
the passing moments
leaving more to chance
than his world could answer for.
I awake
in bits, holding
a furled napkin
to wipe my sweat.
F. wrote a note
to me
in which he explained
that I would inherit his mouth.
I took this
two ways. Asleep again,
I could not remember
what trolley I was to take,
in Moscow.

F. writes a letter to his wife:
Goodbye.
Left in the folly
of a motion
in the hind part
of an alley.

Who goes there becomes
the salvage of his name, as if
        he saw forward
to the faint of his analysis,
dragged like a dead dog over thought's
                apparitions.
    Justice is only
a mood? But he will hold it
        in perpetual
                flarelight.

    F. muddled in dirt, accuses
        the handshake of tyranny,
of vast apostasy in the core
                of friendship.
    Jung exploded him
like a sudden, huge firecracker.
                Synchronicity
        was a special field,
        a practical joke,
        predicated as it was
    against the elder master.
Heaven is loud when the angels
                troop in,
        like gods
                in Wagner's
                Valhalla.
    F. would be lonely now,
not even Anna to hold his mind
in the bowl of her hands.
His years edge closer to his

last case.
Religion is an atheist
commodity.
He is kindest in the moments
after the seas flood his eyes:
he is lyrical.

His friend Lou Salome became
his culture's love goddess,
intellectual temptress,
blackest bread. Gertrude, source
of white words
on ebony dishes.
So time solidifies
in F.'s pen. Gertrude, in Paris,
deifies language as she defies it,
taking it
apart.
His wife saw
to the cooking,
Minna chipped away
at the bronze
case notes.
F. was certainly neurotic. He
transposed passion and exhaustion.
Everywhere the age accumulated
money, seeped into
depression.

F. steps on a cockroach. Later,
simple birds, without memory,
revisit their past

and die.
On another revision
Freud writes:
I will be revised
in the years
long ago. He sleeps in England
before Hitler's war, the first paper
bombs
falling on the land
where he no longer practiced,
where he read life
as already blown up.
He walked
the brain's maze the wrong way,
right-footed,
under mature lightning
and was struck by his own life:
a moebius strip,
the twist of thought
aligned with Thanatos
even as Eros lived,
even as he snuffed out his last cigar.

Falling into Meditation

And it is yesterday again when I fell
asleep while walking,
      then woke into the core
        of a dream,
stretched out without structure,
        believing anyhow
   that I would rise again,
   an ancient man, wearing
         stones.

   Lights flickered around me,
drawing air from a song somewhere
      at a great distance.
   I couldn't identify the words,
     but my mind relaxed
and saw a photograph that looked
more like me than I did. For a moment
I thought my heart was numb, that it beat
      in the hollow
        of a phrase:
    Messiah is no stranger
      to your life.
   And I regarded my sleep as an
         opening
     in slow motion, arms
        plunging
toward the ground to a depth I'd never
     reached before.

   I became a human statue then,
     weathering all weathers,

apropos in any case,
a cast of dice that chance finally won.
And one among many who praised
                    the breath,
               secure
          for a time
     in mortality. When I rose
from the concrete bed, I sailed
          like a paper airplane—
          a Freudian paradox: could I be
                    civilized
               and yet content?

     Shadowy lights followed me
                    everywhere
          during the sun.
I couldn't escape from whatever held me
          in its motherly arms.
This is a gift, this season of birth,
as I stand now among the visible angels,
without falling.